"Michael J S~~eidlinger~~, ~~1~~
Loneliness Package, is a beast! Or rather, a bestiary. ~~Each poem's~~
composed to someone lost to the poet, and as this book accrues,
we discover all that the direct address in a poem can do. This
collection reconciles with a past that is not past, still alive inside
the writer and shows how poetry can be a means of assembling our
ghosts, of reaching across the void into the unknown, regardless of
what you'll find reaching back."
—sam sax, author of *Madness*

"I loved how Michael J Seidlinger's *Standard Loneliness
Package* navigates the ways in which communication and
companionship fail us and leave us longing for more. The speaker
of these poems earnestly traces the silhouettes of different
people from their life, wondering what lingers after the person
is gone. This book is tender and sad, but not without hope—no
matter who this speaker encounters, there's always something
left behind to document, collect, and value."
—Chelsea Hodson, author of *Tonight I'm Someone Else*

"Michael J Seidlinger's *Standard Loneliness Package* begins with
the lines 'The first poem / The first apology / Of a book made /
To haunt me.' The book will haunt you too. Each piece explores,
without reserve, his earliest personal relationships and how
they shape him. This is a collection for anyone who hasn't been
their best self, for anyone hoping to make sense of their own
loneliness, for anyone struggling to accept the mistakes and
misgivings about their past. Seidlinger explores the dark parts
of himself and the people around him with the keen eye and a
generous heart."
—Christine Stroud, author of *Sister Suite*

A Broken River Books original

Broken River Books
12205 Elkhorn Ct.
El Paso, TX 79936

ISBN: 978-1-940885-43-8

Printed in the USA.

STANDARD

Loneliness Package

MICHAEL J SEIDLINGER

POEMS

BROKEN RIVER BOOKS

EL PASO, TX

ALSO BY MICHAEL J SEIDLINGER

FICTION

My Pet Serial Killer
Falter Kingdom
The Strangest
Messes of Men
The Face of Any Other
Mother of a Machine Gun
The Fun We've Had
The Laughter of Strangers
The Sky Conducting

NONFICTION

Mark Z. Danielewski's House of Leaves: Bookmarked

For Rose, Matthew, Joanna, and David—
A challenge given is a challenge met.

To Jami

And the history of the drink
How long does it last
Until it goes bad
Better that you sobered up
While I kept swearing to myself
Each sip will strengthen me
The same way history
Haunts every new face
Every old friend
Every word of disappointment
Healing something nothing
Instead turning you into
The first poem
The first apology
Of a book made
To haunt me

To Ben

Saying you're lonely
Always gave you the perfect excuse

Before we all got together
Whispering that one word—
Intervention

Maybe it was our fault
Which meant it was mine
You were alone

We could be there for you
I could be there for you
But we won't

You probably haven't changed
Have you
I keep texting you

Are you okay

Expecting you to say yes
When you don't say a thing

To Henry

You always said playing music would get you laid
Maybe it did

You were always so good
At pretending

Plagiarizing every line
I learned that from you

Much like every line in this poem
I wrote hearing your voice

Begging me not to tell
The world

You're a fraud

It doesn't matter
It doesn't matter

I'm telling you it doesn't
Because they already know

They knew all along

To Keri

I liked that you listened
To my lies
Not caring at all if they turned
Into something bigger
Mythical was my hope
Miserable was what we were
Every day we promised each other
We weren't afraid
But I was the one that left you behind at that bar
Figuring the day I lose you
Had already passed
When really
I had lost you on the first lie
The very first lie
The blank space of every page
Existing to remind me
Of how emotionally unavailable
I was, and how I could say it so easily
I love you
Another lie
The one thing that should be fact

To Jessica

You sitting two tables down facing me
While I sat with people I hated
But pretended to befriend
Just so I could catch every single look
You tossed my way

Being one for commitment
I kept at it
Even when you put yourself out there
Tried to talk to me, tried to bump into
Me when we passed each other in the hall

And I looked right through you
Negating every chance there may have been
You chose someone else
Someone next to you

How can you be a good actor
How can you fight loneliness
When you turn down every role
When you refuse to try

To Derek

You were the person
I confided in, telling you
My worst fear, the one
That I truly believe

Everyone I choose to know
Everyone I allow to know me
Leaves me

And then you switched topics to the only thing
You ever talked about
Did you hear that some band
Whoever—
What does it really matter
They put out a new album
Did I realize I chose poorly
Add it to my list of ongoing
Poor decisions
I told you when really I should have

Kept those fears
To myself

You don't advertise fear

To Gary

You're going to die anyway

And when I hated the high

Swearing I could do better

Swearing I should do better

You told me I was a ghost

Could see right through me

I looked in the mirror and chanted Bloody Mary

When that didn't work I chanted Candyman

If I am dead

And they showed up to kill

Maybe they would bring me back to life

But nothing happened

The mirror reflects nothing

Is that a smile

No, couldn't be

You were the one that always smiled

I'll never forget what you said

I was the only person you knew

That tried so damn hard to hide

Suppress every single thing

That could make me happy

To May

Just in case you text me
Saying it's okay to move back
Into your life, the apartment full of shelves
We were good at living
Through fiction, just like we were
Better at expressing ourselves
Through the words we would later write
And never show each other

To Eric

You say sorry too much
It loses its effect

I'm sorry
That every single thing I do
I fucked up

In hindsight—
You have a point
What am I doing with my life
The very thing you said about getting your first tattoo

Believing it's forever when one day
It'll fade if you don't go back to get it
Touched up

Much like how we were friends for a summer
But lost touch when neither of us
Lived in the same city, a tattoo
Loses color and meaning
The same way a friendship loses
Feeling after everything
Shared fades and loses focus

I'm sorry that I stopped talking
I'm sorry that I really don't care
I'm sorry that I'm only writing this poem
Because I know you'll never read it
I'm sorry about pretty much everything
But I'm not sorry about this poem

To Jay

Building your body up to be something more
Didn't ever work out well for you did it
Even fought a few matches
Your boxing record something like
Three and two and one
A countdown to yet another disappointment
I lost a lot of money believing in you
I don't care
You lost a lot of money believing in me
I told you not to
It was a good gesture
At the time I explained to you
I go into everything full-hearted
Only to discover that I have only half
I can pretend for only so long
And no, I haven't written
A new song since

To Lawrence

I wondered how often people walked up
And told you how much they dug
What you did, what you no longer do

And I wonder now if they walk up to you more often
Since you quit and began life as another quitter
The fact that you wouldn't tell me, didn't want
To talk about it

Told me everything I needed to know
They never approached you
They just ignored you like everyone else

If I see you again, I'll walk right up
And tell you that I liked your art
Tell you that it changed my life
Just because it might ruin your day
It's the least I can do

To Kyle

Do these words have worldwide appeal
Can one language translate so well
Into another

That it saves itself from losing
Even a modicum of meaning
In the process, because I swear

You got out of the country
At the right time
And if there's any doubt about what you did
It should be only in that we stopped talking
For long enough to let our lives transform
And outlive

We joke about it being the same
Much like how we joke about word count
And what we have left to write
But it has changed

I haven't written enough today
And I'm worried that there's nothing left to write
That eventually I'll give into the idea
That you'll outdo me
Publish and be more productive

And how selfish and horrible it is for me
To have created such a meaningless
Sense of competition

There is no end to this

To Dawn

How I let you down when you tried
To bring me up, a version of capture the flag we played
On summer days melting like the crayons
I left out on the patio

You always told me to stick to the near corners
When I sought out the farthest
Some rebellious display of cowardice
Because it wasn't that I was fearless
I was afraid, I'm still afraid

But I wanted you to see me
I wanted you to capture me in some way
Even now I'm not quite sure
But here was I, so young, a child really
And there you were, old enough to have already been
Let down more than once

And imagine your disbelief
A child, me, barely able to speak
About anything else but *X-Men* cards
Said those words, the kind of thing you tell someone
Right before you ruin their lives

Maybe I did, but you were an adult, and me, a child
You kept babysitting me, us, my sister and cousins
Though we never again played capture the flag
The corners overgrown, the summer days
Quickly melting into fall

To Unknown (#1)

So much of what I did was drink
And do anything to break down my chances
Of seeing you again

What was your name
What was the name of the song you played
On repeat at that bookstore where you clerked

I was the guy that bought books by
Chuck Palahniuk and Douglas Coupland
And kept rambling about South Korean film
Thinking you cared, though maybe you cared

We shared a moment, I'm sure of it
The twinkle of an eye, cliché telling of a typical
Next step, but where there should have been a first date
There was instead a disappearance—
My own

I couldn't bear to see you after having said so much
You saw right through me, I bet
This is how it happens every single time

I never got your name
And you'll never know mine.
How many times before I forget
What it feels like to make a connection
To say to another, Am I worth the risk

I might hurt you
You might hurt me

But let's try, yeah why not
What do we really have to lose

But another block of time
Alone to heal

To Cybil

No was his name, the guy I said was horrible for you
But you went with him anyway

I answered every text and phone call
At 3AM to aid in the destruction
Still hurting from the rejection, a pitiful

And selfish thing that I personalized
Made perfect plan for revenge

Via the friendship I said we could still have
Yeah, we're still friends

How many times have I said that to a person
I no longer trusted
Maybe I didn't think it was this bad

Maybe I really thought it was just hard
Sharing a life is hard
When what you've worked on for yourself

Barely counted as one
Why didn't I ever do anything
I found it fascinating to see you

Courageously filming yourself for him
And then sending me the videos
Asking me if it was okay
Or too much

Trusting that I wouldn't lie

Wouldn't let something so intimate
End up with him

No

Say it: *No*

But I didn't, though I did save the videos
I've watched them at least once since

You stopped seeing him
Stopped seeing me
Stopped seeing everything

To Victor

You shouted best
When you spread each rumor
Like a broken bone jutting out

That one playoff game where
Reality became as real for you
As it always was for everyone else
But you healed up

And people helped with the healing
All the while turning an all-knowing eye
To everyone, like me
That never could score
Never could make the team
No matter what team it was

We walked and talked and wanted to belong
Yet broken bones made for surefire
Weapons of attention
And of accentuating just how little
A person like me had compared to you

You got that scholarship
You got the girl
You made sure to get me every day in the hallway
Between 2nd and 4rd period
And while the day ended and you moved on
I held it in, all of it

Wishing I could score and shout with the best of them
Which you believed was entirely you

There is an "I" in team

And the entire school knew
I was the last to admit it
A bloody nose does more than ruin a shirt

To Scott

If I remembered you longer than a day
We'd be good friends
You took to the trail, walking

The east coast, pretending that somehow
You'd end up west
As far away from the mother that hit you
And the father that forced you to get drunk
With him so that he wouldn't feel lonely

But the gas station, just a shitty Shell station
Was where our past and future died
And in the ether we accentuated each moment
With another band we discovered
Another song to play, another show to attend
Every mosh pit was our last

You scared me to death with the stories you told
About people getting trampled
When the only real trauma was outside
Those crowds

Away from those densely packed show floors
When the song started and the circle pit spun
We were two friends
Running away from the image of who we would become

Are you still running
Did you ever slow down or crawl
Some nights I can still see that scared kid
Some nights I think it's still 1998

To Oliver

You told me the best thing I wrote
Was a book that never made it to store shelves
Not even a single review
But what does it matter, you said
Every book written is one step closer to being forgotten
In defiance I wrote nothing for six months
You finished a novel and fell asleep one night
The next morning you were a new person
No one understood
But getting into Harvard shut them up
But not me
I'm right here
Asking for the real you
Where are you buried
So that I can dig you up
Though I can't save myself
I know that I can save you
Just tell me where
Tell me where

To William

We were eating freshly fallen snow
Though you were a manager of a corporate chain
At the grocery store, high on methamphetamines
And I was whoever the fuck I am
Drunk on the prospect of getting drunker

You told me that you wanted to kill yourself
I told you to do it one better
Kill someone else
You grinned
I danced around the fact that it was a joke
I wasn't being serious
But then you asked me about my situation
And I didn't need to say anything
I looked the part

He asked how long since the last
He inquired if she broke up with me
I didn't say anything
Which is code for yes
And then he took the first mouthful of snow
And I followed suit
After a few mouthfuls, we didn't make any sense
Our mouths frozen, our voices silenced

But later, only later, when I was warm and worn down
In bed with the same books
Watching the same episodes of *The Simpsons*
I understood what you had told me
You're lucky, you'll be okay as long as you
Forget what it feels like to be alone

To James

They were all so happy, you said
As we watched jealously from the rafters
Like this was still high school
Like we weren't twenty going on twenty-one
Those were the middle years
The meddling ones when we kept to the same clan
K and c and j and b
Names I don't remember much
But it was music, only music that we never made
But talked about so often
While being obsessed about the moments
Our rebellion had denied
You go to prom
You'd talk about how stupid it was with confidence
You going to college
You'd talk about how much time was wasted on tuition
I never called you out
Never mentioned that these middle years cost us five
The difference being that if I had gone to prom
I'd at least had the awkward kiss the awkward stumble
The awkward chance that never was
Instead it was erased, and where the diploma should be framed
I have a few scars and a blank slate
The aftertaste of a life that never was
I don't hear any music
Do you

To Lauren

You always wanted to be a part of my story
Or a chapter, maybe a line, or better yet
A character memorable enough
For the few that ever bothered to read

Well, I'm not sure if you ever found immortality
And I'm not sure you're still looking between the pages
But I'll tell you, *There's nothing there*
So what does that mean, then, if you turned each page
Hoping to be hidden, somehow lost and transformed
Somewhere between chapter seven and chapter eight

Well it's taken awhile for me too, a dozen books
More than a hundred odd hooks aiming to fight off rejection
But I'm moving away from the book smell
And the allure of being able to point to a bookshelf and say
That book's mine
And have it mean more than, *Hey I bought that book*
You wanted me to write you
I wasn't a writer then

And I'm not sure I'm a writer now
But I've been walking this road long enough to know
That no one's going to write you

To Jeff

At that *Decemberists* show I couldn't see your face
The lighting in the room dim
But could hear you
Above the distortion
I hoped that there wasn't any mystery
Behind the reason we went to the show
You could have gone with someone else
We should have invited more than just you and me
But here, young enough that we had to wear
The black sharpie x's on the back of our hands
I stood leaning against the barricade
Wishing the band opening was better
You leaning into me
Wishing I would have felt the same
Way you felt about me
Instead I led you on
Days after, maybe weeks
You took it lightly
Long enough to have a day's lead
Before the sequence where
I realized it was my fault
That you moved to Italy
And the vanity of believing
It was due to a broken heart
Ten years later, I still can't see your face
But that has nothing to do with my memory
More so you wanting nothing to do with me

To Unknown (#2)

Saying I live in this room
For me doesn't mean a bed and a desk, a couple
Tosses and turns or a lean at a desk with a cup of coffee
It means hiding
To be closer to you

It means locking the world out
The door and walking the town
Living in this room
Means knowing its every shape and texture
Means knowing the room so well
It becomes an extension of my body

Living in this room
Means every smell, every motion, every
Single activity is mine
You can't be lonely
If the edge of your world is a locked door
And a closed window

I've sat here listening to the rain
So long I hear nothing else
If this is what it feels like to be alone
Perhaps what I'm really trying
To do is be closer to you

To Stephanie

It was so hot we spooned naked
Figuring if we had to feel the heat
It might as well be the heat of each other's bodies
Fear being that you'd have another seizure

Or that I would get bored
I always got bored
Maybe not today, how about tomorrow
The cadence to my excuse
Was the catastrophe of your reaction
Knowing that I was the disappointment
Of the day, the disappointment of our time together
A month, two if you count the time
After we stopped talking

But still showed up
And fucked
And spooned
Never bothering to say a word
Especially simple things like
Be well
And
Hope you're okay
We just were
And then we weren't
And I think of you now mostly
Based on how you smelled between
Those sheets

To Andy

You didn't say much until you were ready to slam a person
Everything hate and some other variety of harm
But it was good
It was a time to be angry
Everything good ended
And loneliness ran deep in your life
And mine, it had been that way for a while
Before we met at the practice space
You, looking for a band
Me, looking to leave my current band
Here's what's wrong with that band
Here's what's wrong with that album
Here's what's wrong with you
Here's what's wrong with
Don't talk about mine
It was all you
You talked
I smoked and took the pills you found
And then we wrote music
With a few other members of local bands
Everyone lonely, everyone tired
Everyone sticking around the practice space
Because there wasn't anything else
I'll never forget that time we managed to write
Two songs only to discover that they were derivative
Of a band we both hated

To Danielle

This is why I don't date
I said
This is why I do nothing but date
You said
But sadness was the plan
A Tinder date that turned into something lesser
Or better

At a later date, all I know is you're currently
The top three most frequently texted
We met at some midtown restaurant
May I take your jacket, I said
And you laughed
High strung because I was nervous
I go cold and numb when every emotion fights to be felt
You broke the ice and then asked for a bucket
And two bottles of white wine

We'll eat somewhere else, you said
That was a big deal
Denying the establishment
We walked rather than taking the train
Twenty-nine blocks
Before making it to your apartment
Nobody was home, except us
We ordered in
And we talked until dawn
We're still talking
Consider this poem layaway for when
We no longer are

To Maori

Call me after ten and I'll be drunk
Even if you told me you'd call then
And it was a big deal, the next step in your life
Meanwhile my own stagnated a year ago
Just enough to engage the backslide
Into a textbook case of loneliness
You called and the next day I didn't remember
But it was what you needed

All you needed to sign on the dotted line
I talked to you later, when you won that award
And you thanked me personally

You asked if I was jealous
No, I said

I told you the truth

Stressing just how rare that was
The truth saying, I can't believe I'm being thanked
More than that, I can't believe it

Believe what, you sounded so concerned
I must have sounded insane
But see, what are the chances that a person
Can get used making a positive difference in another person's life
You did your best to explain it to me
Just like I did my best to congratulate you and get as quickly off
The phone and away from you as possible

I'm saying it here, it wasn't you

Rather the first time I blacked out
I changed saved a person's life
That can't be good
For me, that might just spell

Doom

To Ingrid

Yeah you were nobody
Never worth a damn, just a name attached
To a number I never called
Or maybe I did

But these were the early days of an art form
Every song I wrote was a fantasy of every
Single person I'd turn on
How cliché could I be
Yeah, well, you too
The difference between you and I
Is that we still talk, we still text at 5AM
When we're afraid that morning will never come

I ask you now though, sincerely
What was in those blue baggies
And why did we never see Ashley again
Was it you, or was it me
I'm all questions whenever we talk
You're all confirmations and dates and times

Come here if you want to get laid
I'm still stupidly and arrogantly proud
That I never took you up on the offer
Even when I gave you $300 to help
And you offered it for free

To Reagan

We sat for weeks
Side by side pretending to be too busy
With our work to talk to each other, nothing
Not even a little glance

I caught your name off the top right of a term paper
Our first words were more a motion
You handing me the joint, me handing you my phone
Me asking you via text if you wanted to
You telling me in a series of emojis

Telling me that you had thought about it all semester
After it was a dorm room, yours or mine
It didn't matter
I still carry it with me, the very definition of what it feels
Like to regret
Something that can't be taken back
And I'm so sorry that it's you

You were so happy that I willfully gave three months
Of my life, a relationship and breakup, just to be sure
That when I broke your heart, it made sense
Somehow thinking breaking it at the end
Of a relationship was somehow easier than doing it right
Then and there

Perhaps when it was still nothing more
Than a one-night-stand
Maybe I was covering for myself
I wasn't ready to see you go

To Ashley

I have no idea where you went
No idea where you've gone
But if you ever see this
Reading this thing
Standard loneliness package
A book full of apologies and regret
Call me, text me – 410 598 3485
Email me – fieldsandfractures@gmail.com
Please, just tell me
You're okay

To Christine

And all the times, too many times
I told you that you talked too much
And drank too much, essentially more than me
Enough of a reason to fall in love with you

My first time, your fifth
Maybe I hated that you didn't think much at first
Not that you said those words
That I assumed were the truth
And I went back to assuming
I wasn't good enough
That was the extent of it, wasn't it

But after a hundred parties and the inevitable
Sitting around on a Friday night at home
We dashed for the kitchen knives
And you cut me good
I couldn't do it, though I put on a show of it
In the ambulance, we didn't say anything

The hospital room in and out of consciousness
You sat there, never said a thing
On the cab ride back home, never said a thing
The following morning, the bandages still flecked
With blood as you moved the six or seven boxes, your stuff
Into your car
Never said a thing
When you drove off, the music blaring, moments after heading
Down the street, I never said a thing

To Quinnie

Late nights watching horror flicks
When we should have been afraid
Of what was happening outside our window
But we were so perfect for each other
Weren't we, we drew each other
Wrote an entire comic series together
You as the main character
Me as the antagonist
We escaped from the protests outside
What lasted little more than a week
Though the uncoiling our emotions
The protests we shared, who cared more
And who would leave first
Lasted four times as long
I'll never forget how we stood there
Your skin, the hair on my arms standing
On end
The way you turned around and said the words
How I was already so nervous
That when I looked down
And saw that I was hard
It was all we needed, to commit to the decision
The one so right yet so wrong
The hero of this story is the one that stands up for herself
When the antagonist starts talking about a future
Where there's very little her, the talk about going on tour,
The discussion about her going too
I didn't expect you to go, but hoped that you would
When you didn't, and stayed behind, I knew that you won
Though we never said goodbye
We never broke up

We never finished our comic series
Just like we never finished watching *X-Files*
The hero escapes while the antagonist is left
To forever wonder, which is all
I ever really do honestly

To Tom

Everything was a videogame
Where it was mandatory that you won
Even loneliness
Where you steeled your nerves for those
Moments and days when color went black and white
The weight of every minute felt like the usual weight of an hour
On a day that's a lesser shade of gray
Those minutes that render living
Life itself
So painful and explicit
One never feels more alive
Than when they understand how alone they are
In the world that continues unabated
With or without your participation
You could, and have, wait all year indoors
Hiding from the world
It'll never hide from you though
A notification on your phone revealing
How happy and satisfied everyone else
You know is at this very moment
The moment when you know you could hold your breath
Long enough to never again have to breathe

To Heather

Who majored in humanities
But set her PHD in loss
And specifically breakup

We haunted those library halls
With what it means to be alone

You believed that being lonely was merely a half step
From being alone
Whereas I told you that I was your best bet
The one person that has been alone so often
That you couldn't call me lonely
If you wanted

And the drugs you bought, I ended up taking
Under the bed rather than on it
You found me there
Laughing and falling to the floor
I kissed the bruise and every blemish for a year
Before you finally defended your thesis
And what I told you became true
The faults bringing down years of work
We did our best to stay the same

Then you into a darkness I wasn't ready
To dive back into
Until the next novel
But we said goodbye with an hour consisting of
Smoke and fire and prolonged embraces
I said the words, I love you

But you told me you couldn't say it back
Until you believed the same for yourself
Did you ever defend your thesis successfully
Did you ever prove that loss is permanent

To Jade

All we ever talked about was loneliness
It seemed ironic to have gotten so close
Discussing the very thing that we glorified

I wanted to be alone
More than that, I believed I deserved
To be lonely
Though I wasn't

But then we sat at tables
Our hands inching closer and closer
And suddenly our loneliness
Became our love
The glow of the screen sometimes blinds me
In the same way our brief infatuation
Blinded me

To the root of the problem
Eventually we knew we'd leave
Returning like the night
Into the far corner where we preferred to dwell

To Kevin

You remember it well—
The studio late at night, identical
To the early morning
The same producers and designers
Disguising their own disgruntlement
The mainstays were the ones

That wanted the worst
Of us that were there because being so
Meant we never had to be ourselves
Here, where the hum of high end workstations drowned out
Any wayward thoughts, you told me

Never to tell anyone else but
I have to, I've kept it secret for too long
Much longer than we were friends
But it haunted me, the fact that you decided to tell me
Instead of someone else that cared
Expecting me to be there, when you knew that I wouldn't

I was like everyone else in the studio
Looking out for my own interests
I couldn't have cared if your dad gave you those
Bruises or whether or not you had been homeless and needed help
The studio kept people in roles, contained

Making them less human
In doing so, somehow liberating us into telling total strangers
Being saved by the telling alone

To Anne

We met on a deathbed

She reached for me instead of you

Nicole and I had only been dating a month when it happened

Rushing to the hospital, I was a nervous wreck

I hadn't met the parents

And now I'd meet one in the form of an embrace

Meant for one of her daughters

Go figure, I was awkward

I was pulling away the moment she passed

And nicole did more than cry and blame me

She still blames me, but you didn't

I knew you just wanted me to tell you what your mother said

Explain in explicit detail what she looked like

At the very last blink

I hoped those lunch dates were truly dates

And when we kept seeing each other, never in an official capacity

I tried to embrace you the same way your mom did

Tried to pass it on to you, but just enough

Just enough to be able to truly know you

And for you to know me, move on to hopefully being more

Than a strange couple weeks stuck in time

To Grant

Tree lined streets and the feeling
That nothing new will ever happen

We ended up in the dense silences
Of the middle class at rest
You found in me the friend

You needed and I found in you another voice
Added to the worry
The worry that turned out to be true

I am better than this
I am better than you
It killed me to think of it

How does it feel to have been the one bad seed
While in wait everyone is wondering
Why these two young men are wasting
Their lives

To Meredith

We told each other to stop watching
First act in the film called forever
Where we wore the tropes like masks

They couldn't come off and we didn't want them to
The chance meeting at a party, the matchmaker friend
That turned out to be jealous of you, of me, of both of us
Second act in a film called forever

The first kiss was followed by a dozen others, the firsts of many
On the same night we decided to last a year
Surprise adventures, spontaneity, the thought that it couldn't get
Any better, but could always get worse, yet scene after scene
We outdid each other

And the pacing was absolutely perfect
Third act in a film called forever
We have a fight, maybe two, in the same week
Montage about the little things, conveniently forgetting
The particulars followed by a scene that's missing
And a would be final act

But we call it quits, we disband the entire set
Knowing where the direction was heading
We'll still be friends, it's better that way
A partial script becomes a number of dates rescheduled
And I'm the one that looks to cast someone else for your role
We told each other to stop watching

We agreed, it would be devastating
But you see, I never really was recording

To Leigh

I always wore headphones
To hide from people
To avoid having to ever
Look eye to eye and on the spot
Forced to acknowledge another person's existence
You see it was a weird time
When is it ever a not a weird time
But I was in a weird place and I was really interested
Wanting so very much to at least have you know my name
We inhabited this building throughout those first semesters
Of college, when I was at my loneliest
Around so many people, and yet having no one
You made it worse, my imagination using you as a stand-in
For everything I was missing
I called the dorm room my reprieve
Seldom leaving unless to find food or attend class
I told myself I was writing but really I hadn't written a thing
Guess it's my way of saying, I wish I met you, wish it could have
Worked out differently, how, I don't know what
But at least some version where I don't have to erase
My freshman year of college from memory

To Emma

When you're alone and worse
Lonely, the sort of lonely that slows down
The shortest breaths, the simplest of motions
You can't be sure when life starts
Everything feels lesser framed
There isn't a lot to say
So you post pictures extensively online

And people like, comment, and follow you
I know it helped, you told me
No, you didn't have to say anything
It could be seen in every interaction online
You said what you didn't mean to say
And I followed your photography
Watching it take hold, ending up featured
When suddenly it all stopped

I kept checking but you stopped posting
A couple months ago you deactivated everything
Though it made me feel as lonely as you felt
Knowing you're gone, part of me pretends that you
Found a solution, someone to love, a life that ensures that you
Never have to feel that way again, but if that's the case
I kind of wish you'd keep

Everything online, they were for many, a solemn reminder
That others feel just as disconnected
But then I wondered if you did it on purpose

Every part of it a performance

And if so
This is why
It's so hard
To know
Someone

To Alyssa

To you there was always a puppy
The two so competitive, vying for your every affection
Others that lingered long after you let go
Of their leash

And then there was me, who sat down instead of running
Looked up instead of growling
Into those eyes that changed color
Depending on the mood, depending on the day
What did you see in mine

Other than a dull brown, a blink and then another frown
Old wine and a late night watching cartoons
Up all night talking, making sense of where our lives
Went wrong

Disclaimer—I will push you away
Disclaimer—I will hurt you

Held to so many disclaimers, earliest of discussions
The material typically saved for brutalist breakups
But we had our year, and we could have been like puppies
Growing old together, but instead I growled, I snapped

This wasn't the place, this wasn't the place
Maybe if we were, or maybe if it was more like this
Excuses—I love you but
The word is enough, but

It keeps us at bay

And so you went, and maybe I went long ago
But some days, the better days, I feel you so near
And this is me telling you every apology

To Romeo

Six in the morning you would already be barking
I hated and liked everything about it
The routine of a morning walk, followed by food
followed by my two hours to write

Before once again being forced out, a walk, *Do your business*
Back inside for more work while you would stare at me
Sitting in some far corner, just visible enough so that whenever
I looked

You would be there, looking at me in wonder
Understanding that I was projecting the guilt onto you
Day after day, more of the same, the pressure of the deadline

I'm not happy about what I did, but pulled at all ends
I had to do the same to you, leaving you in a crate all day
One walk, one chance for food and to "do your business"

This happened for a week before desperation kicked in
When I got the news, it wasn't the end of the world
But it sure felt like it
The deadline I fought, the book I had written, rejection
I was young then

I wasn't thinking about anyone else but myself

So I left the house
And walked four miles to the nearest gas station
Bought a few boxes of wine
And walked the same four back

It started in the driveway
And didn't end until I was blacked out in the basement
The clock, when I came to, was four in the afternoon
Two days later

I retraced my steps, the hangover still one of the worst I've felt
And I found you there, still in your crate
Days worth of shit, piss up to just
Above your paws, and you, matted hair and shivering

You wouldn't trust me for weeks after
Even when your owner returned
And when you finally let me pet you, I didn't trust myself

To Abby

I could teach a class on distance
You taught a class on getting to know people

We met during the third session
It took skipping the first two to get me there
And another thirty minutes to keep me from walking out
But you saw right through me

Getting that I didn't want to participate
Sitting in the back and listening
The only one that didn't share a story

You ignored me and in doing so you did more
Than anyone could at that time
After class, in the parking lot

You left a note
One I still haven't read

To Peter

I got the email, and after a few days
I emailed you back

Sure enough, it was as you wanted
Here's everything I've done with my life

Make me out to be exact, make me a disgusting monster
I still regret saying yes but it was a Saturday night

When I got to chatting with you via email, and said yes
I said yes, and you gave me what you had, notes upon notes

I shuddered at what you had done
Discussions among friends about involving the authorities

But we were all cowards, and more so, I thought about my own
Safety so I deleted all the files off my hard drive

And ignored all of your emails
For weeks, you continued to contact me

I started up a new email address out of desperation
Only to come back to 63 unread emails from you

Well I've been wanting to tell you
I read them, I read them and it hurts me so much

To say this but, you're the only person that I sincerely
Regret ever knowing

At least you got the help you needed
At least you agreed to the charges

To Jesse

We never really said anything, rather you'd write a phrase
And I would reply, both of us consulting the books we had
Which eventually led us to discussing every word
Every line written on yours wasn't like what was in mine
The word, meaning—
How difficult it is to truly communicate to someone

It wasn't easy for us

At least I got sentimental and said things like
At least it means I'm never truly alone

To Casey

In the shower, you tell him to get out
Every day for two months you've showered together
But not today
And in the kitchen later, you make a meal for one
He tries to pick a fight when he sees an empty plate

But you're already outside, and walking
You're outside and talking
To me, who walks next to you
Before we get to our respective buildings

But you told me, that morning
A few things that stuck with me
A few things about being a human
Like how a person needs time to be a person

There is only you
Standing there wishing someone would tell you
How—but maybe, just maybe, a person needs
To be lonely

To Mitch

Did I ever tell you that
You are my own worst enemy

Of course I didn't
But it's true
Which is shitty because you
Are nice to me
You're nice to everybody
But that makes me hate you more
Because you rub it in

You make sure in your own little way
That I know that I'm the one
That'll be alone

To Shawn

If there is a rock bottom
And I've known it
What do you call where you've been

The things you've seen
Forced to give away what you had
Forced to look in every single person's eyes
And say, I'm sorry

But still, it doesn't prevent you from ending up
Where you started—naked, empty, and penniless
So if you do this more

Than once, I have to wonder
Are you searching or looking
To become ironman

To Caroline

When I asked the manager, he told me you were transferred
To another store, so then I asked if it was by choice
He looked at me, and I knew
Still, to this day, I hold it in me
A notch turning and tightening like so many
Other broken ties

To Allison

To touch your skin was to feel three decades
Gone awry, your face as pretty as it possibly ever was
Marked only by the choice, your own
To carve a line across your right cheek
I asked you, the first time we met, why you did it
Citing principles of body modification, I was silenced
Knowing my question had an answer that was yours to keep
We talked late into the night, at that bar, past closing
But you knew the bartender, and we talked
Dancing around what wasn't really there

The invitations began days later, never from you
Always from the venue, and I saved and eventually tossed
Them all, embarrassed for thinking that the invites
Were from you, instead of just some mailing list

To Ian

Why didn't I listen to you
When you told me
You were destined for great things
This won't take long
You said that
But me, I was the one person that walked on
Not listening, only later seeing that you
Dropped a card in my front pocket
Name, twitter, email, et al
The recipe for jealousy
That would start six months later

To Jonathan

Do you know, I bet you don't
But do you know that every single time
Every single time
You knocked on my door
Or tried to use a credit card
To get into my room
I was there
Did you
I bet you didn't

To Morgan

There was a fire down the street one night
And we were neighbors in a tired old suburban neighborhood
The biggest excitement was the fire itself
and whether there were people left inside
We debated about whether people should go inside to check
The firefighters weren't there yet

And I wasn't destined to be even remotely heroic
But when people around us started listening
They brought us clothing and we became swept into the act
Six, maybe seven layers I hoped were at least a little fireproof
I led the way but not because of anything in particular

Truth is I lost sight of you, in those smoking halls
And the dark billowing clusters that felt so heavy
I could have fallen right then and there
I walked and looked and found nothing
So I cowardly left, but you, you were there longer
Long enough that I started back in
Where I found you was in the back
Not with someone fallen but rather
You gathering jewelry, a fortune
The look you gave me

I turned and walked away
A week later, after the fire out of the question
And the family that owned it
Started gossiping about the settlement for some faulty wiring
I must have passed by your house a hundred times
Just wondering if you got out
If somehow I missed my chance

To Keija

And how you always changed your name
With the seasons, turning into someone else

So then it was disconcerting when you were the one
To ask me, every time we met, Why do you want to escape

We could be in the grocery store, looking for something to eat
At some point you would ask me, *Why do you want to escape*

I took it personally and started working on my rebuttal
I must confess, it wasn't much—Why must you change
Stay right here, I wanted to tell you

Be "keija," be here with me
Long enough to be able to know
What it feels like to have seen something—
Be a person with me

I say this knowing well how many times I've changed
In order to avoid trauma, but
You're already be somebody else

To Claire

Yours is the poem I don't know how to write

To Hannah

There was a bag packed from the beginning
Honoring your wishes
We never stood still, never in place but
Long enough to note where we had arrived
in every major American city

Followed by the areas upstate and beyond
The places less visited but far more comfortable
And when we found those we traversed the national parks
Drove the web of interstates before choosing to go
At the last minute, north to Canada rather than south
Mexico, and there you fell into a depression

Because we lost track of time and our momentum
Collapsed, much like my own checking account
Little left, I sold some of my own belongings
And you sold your car, which later became a key point
In an argument, you sold your car to get us to the UK

But we never did, get to the UK I mean
I finally took that step back, at the last minute
During boarding, like out of some clichéd flick
But the difference her is that you didn't look back
You never looked back

You and I were no longer walking side by side
You told me later your secret
About the bag
You never touched it
Everything packed stayed where it was

To Josh

You were always alone
Despite all the parties you've held
You were always standing alone, standing tall
As yourself to the most impressive extent
But I can't help but notice you've never held someone
Close—never had someone by your side, perhaps to share
Your life with them, making it even grander
Than it already is

I wish I could be so confident and invulnerable
Able to navigate this life alone
The way you have, with such relative ease

To Sarah

You won't read this poem
Because you don't actually exist
Instead a composite of characteristics
Formulated during pockets of slow time
Fashioning together the best of everyone
I wronged, everyone I lost
And everyone I will lose
There is you
The idea that loneliness
Has its own rightful end
Which is worth its own weight
In sadness because to have created you
Is enough proof to note that loneliness
Is all encompassing, that
A person can never
Truly escape

To Gabriel

Why didn't you ever tell me
That you were upset about that one post
I will not name

Why did you unfriend me across social media
Erasing yourself everywhere

To Charlotte

Love poem
Because you wanted one
Something I never wrote
In the year and half we were together

The less I see of you
The more I think about moving on

What to think vs what to feel
Because you're no longer here
The feelings we made vs the feelings we faked

I didn't give you a rose on valentines day
And it was reason for you to end it right there

Dinner reservations and a whole night
But there wasn't a rose, and there wasn't a love poem
And there wasn't a romantic spotlight dance
In the ballroom of your cousin's wedding

But you had all these ideas, which I then used for a novel
Which failed, much like us

I'd say I miss you but I know you wouldn't listen
Even though I write this out of forgiveness, a sincere apology

I know, I really do know
But I really need to get one thing off my chest

You always said you'd feel miserable knowing that
People you aren't with are better off without you

I'm here to say that they are, they've moved on
I've moved on, and if you don't want them to live better

Just because you, as a couple, never worked out
Maybe you deserve to sit it out, and understand
That by saying you're lonely, it doesn't mean
There'll be someone there to love you

To Dania

I don't remember any of my childhood friends
Except for you, who might have been the first
The way we couldn't bear to be around anyone
So young and already anxious and explicitly aware
Of the dangers of knowing someone

They'll try to figure you out, they'll try to get to know you
They'll likely end up hurting you
Maybe leaving right when you need them most
But when you and I met, we became fast friends

Funny how I remember us
The various clubhouses and pillow forts and random
Games we made without every really saying much

I miss being able to be around someone without feeling anxious
I miss being able to communicate so much without saying a word
I think I miss you too, but I can't be sure if I'm doing it again—

Cannibalizing memories, trying to nullify my emotions
Thinking foolishly that by feeling nothing
I'll somehow become fearless

To Brandon

I've written three books about what happened between us
None of them published, none of them to ever make any sense
To anyone that might read
Especially me

There's too much that needs to be off the record, too much
That might ruin us if people knew about the late night lurking
The desperate things a person does to make some money
But then nobody probably cares, because like these books

It's all fiction anyway

And you're just a name, a thought that comes to mind
An imaginary friend that I kept, and relied on, during moments
When the loneliness pulled me into another heavy blanket
You'd be there, all confident and full of crazy, fun ideas

And still, I'm not sure you're real, or that any of this
My memories, the loneliness I almost always carry with me
Is something manufactured, a mental illness that has come
To define me

To Philip

People say they'll die in bed
Die in a car accident, just like you did
Being so jealous, so disappointed in your death
I'm sorry

Because I'm more likely to die
By my thoughts, pulling me from the present
And showing me how to stay gone
From the reality that never made sense

Stay there, where I can create
Everything I could never find

To Ruth

Which is a name meaningless to me
Attached to no one in particular
Just the name I use when I think of everyone I'll never know

And depending, a name
I attach to those I've saved, the thought process
Being, You're lucky that you never really have to know me

Because it's that sort of self-deprecation that lingers
Like a redundant phrase in a poem that needs to be revised
At the end of anything that might have been positive

Pretty sure and plainly fact—have a good day
You look good, where did you get that shirt
New haircut, you know how rare it is to see you smile

Things, stupid things, all adding up to a mountain
Of doubt that leaves me defeated, and so the name
I apply to anyone of which I choose to be unavailable

Is you, and a letter of apology, prewritten
For the moment when I disappoint you

To Tim

Because I'm stubborn and an asshole

1) I sabotaged that one piece of yours, giving you bad advice
2) Fact that you can't help yourself
Can't stop drinking once you've started
Didn't stop me from influencing you to get drunk
When I felt ashamed about being the only one that isn't sober
3) Though you pretty much have been one of the most reliable
people I've never actually met, I still don't trust you
And really, I get competitive, I get jealous
And then I get angry at myself for feeling this way
Same as always, which proves to me I'm predictable, repetitive
Haven't been working on myself enough to make those changes
To be a person that isn't broken
In a state of continual despair

But here's 4), the last
I have over a dozen unread messages in
Facebook chat from you that I've read and marked unread
Doing my best to push you away, the best thing I could do
Is push you away, but still, you have messaged me
And you're messaging me right now
I'm sorry but I'm not going to respond
I'm not going to respond but its also unfair
To block you

To Unknown (#3)

Why do I worry if these poems will be published
Do I quantify every single thing I care about
It is true
Every poem is an apology
It is true
Every apology is a poem I have trouble reading aloud
It is true
Every time I apologize
What I'm doing is hiding behind
The fact that I don't know how to change
How to heal
How to show you that I can do better
It is true
This is the best I can do
It is true
The best I can do is never enough
It is true
To keep those I want close
It is true
To distance myself from those I shouldn't keep

To Nick

Just be yourself
I said that
You said the rest, _____
The most important part
The feature about how you could only ever

Really be yourself when no ones around
When no ones watching

Meaning that empty practice space on 5th
The dusty lending library on _____

No one there, no one cares
He she it a pronoun you searched for
When I preferred to call you by name

_____

But the identity that was yours was never
The identity that clung to, _____
Having been used for the first few decades of your life
Just be yourself

It was all I could say, _____
Without admitting that I too had looked
I too had been hidden, by choice
By the longing to be myself

Learning at such a young age
That it was only possible in silence

To Janice

There is this idea I've kept hold of
In the years since we've met, and become
Twin pistons of a single machine

With emotions weighing down on us so often, so heavily
Talk of coffee and pizza and continuing the trek
We're both taking, despite seeing so many back away

This poem isn't about us
So much as it is about the conditions of our parole
Too many voices calling out for us, our attention
When really we just want to hit mute

The idea I'm getting at is that maybe, just maybe
We continue because we actually need this
The work overrunning our lives
Clocking in as continual exhaustion
We need this in order to numb, and neutralize
The emotions and the worry
And the various demons that we fight, this is our fight

Because, I guess the idea really is:
If we're too busy working on the needs
Of others, we'll never be fully aware of what we truly need
It's a scary thought, one that I hope you know
For you at least, isn't true

Because I'll be here, for you, when things threaten to collapse
I'll be there, a single text, phone call, or dog emoji away
From compassion and the words, *We're coping*

To David

Everyone tells me we're exactly alike
Which makes sense, I guess
But part of me is mortified

It can't be true, I have a few more chances
I won't, no, I won't—I can't, and it saddens me
To think this of you, to look at you as
What I never want to become

If it's true or not—we're both sitting at computers right now
Both looking into the lines written for meaning in our lives
Both backsliding into loneliness

Whenever things with people never worked out
If it's true or not—we're both idealistic
Rife with ambition for fostering some sort of legacy
But that's where you stopped and I continue
That's where you never figured it out and me

I'm ready to pretend that I did if it means never
Ever ending up the way you did
It's not over, you might tell me
But I'm here to to say that it is

To Crystal

Imagine me gone and I'll imagine I never met you
Imagine me erasing some of the best moments of my life
Imagine the stairs beneath where one world ended

And another began
We called ourselves enemies
So that when we finally won over each other, it was considered
A victory, the reward being to spend a few months
Of pure naïve emotional bliss
Without ever knowing what it would feel like
When we turned our backs, showing the bruises
Left from our quarrels in bed

And the art we'd create, shunned by so many
As odd and obscure, being like a homing beacon
Bringing us to tears, every time we tried
To forget each other, stillborn as it was

To Nox

The band not the brand
The band not any one person in particular
Just wanted to say wassup
How's it going
Did that whole record deal work out or not
Because I don't see you on Spotify or anywhere else
And hey, yeah, maybe I'm just loving the fact that it didn't
Work out, I mean
Shit went down, I bet
Like to think it was because I left
Probably not but, just want to get it out there
I really hope it was
Know that I'll probably say it was
And personalize the whole messy disbanding
Because I'm like that, weak willed when emotions are high
And it helps to build a fantasy
When reality threatens to wear you down
So yeah, how'd that all go down
Things going well now
Yeah, I bet not right
I mean, really, who am I even talking to

To Rei

You taught me how to sing
And more so taught me how to listen
You listen so well, so much that you knew when I was sad
Long before
Voice starting to crack, whole days where I went hoarse
Voice changing in such a way that everything you taught me
No longer worked
You taught me how to sing
Which is why now whenever I think of you
All I can do is breathe in, breathe out heavily
Heart skipping a beat, nerves tensing
Mind going blank at the thought that
A breath of fresh air has nothing to do with relief

To Damien

You got a lot going for you
Nothing is ever wrong and everything is on-point
Say exactly what is appropriate, just enough
To leave them wanting more
You dress well (except no one knows you only have one suit)
The impression is that you're a real social butterfly
Able and aware, everyone knows you
It's all designed to be an enigma
Your brand is built to allure
To conjure a sense of curiosity in others
So that when I'm feeling down, all I do is become you
And I walk out that front door a different person
Flimsy and performative, the deft eye able to
See right through it
Still I commit to the bit
Even when they gather together
Attempting to exorcise you
Claiming intervention
We know that it's a hard time
We want to help
Why do I need help
I'm Damien

To Unknown (#4)

Is it wrong to stay home
Why is it wrong to stay home
Why do we try so hard
Pay so much
To find home
Only to squander it
And run away
Preferring piss soaked alleys
To the comfort of home
So quickly we devalue where we turn
When we need help
Need to be ourselves
Home is where the heart is
Then why don't I hear a heartbeat

To Unknown (#5)

You almost deleted this entire collection
It's perhaps what I prefer
You would like that wouldn't you
It's the reason I won't

To Unknown (#6)

Suicidal ideation as meditation

Suicidal ideation as common means of word association

I think I have a problem

Feels good to say it, but I should probably seek help

Saying it isn't enough, but there are so many moments

Imagined to be my last, and it used to be writing

Would help curb the fixation

But now it's all I ever write about

Suicidal ideation as topic

I know I have a problem

And it doesn't make me special, or any different

Than any other person lonely on this earth

Clamoring to make sense and keep up

With the life that feels so exhausting at times

Suicidal ideation is a form of relief

I mean, how can a person not think about it

We all think about it and we all have issues

Not as easy as it seams just speaking up and talking to someone

And when life moves so quickly, and the quicksand of

Responsibility pulls you under, its exhaustion maybe

That finally gets a person

To Olivia

What will I say to you when we meet
Should amend that to "if" we ever meet

Because you are merely the person that gets me
The person that's out there for me, that sentimental
Thought that there's someone out there for everyone
But I'm too much of an absurdist

To believe in it
So I fake it, pretending, creating a shadow figure
That carries your name, it's kind of frightening, as time passes
And new wrinkles, new blemishes, now pains

Arise from this body
There is nobody out there meant for you
No sense of destiny that isn't designed and fought for

And time passes ever more, success and failure, a series
Of ups and downs, but I keep it on the cusp of every
Quiet moment, the thought that maybe you do exist

And it's my own emotional unavailability that'll do it
Keeping us from ever meeting and from ever
Being happy

To Mike

I don't forgive you
Having written this book
Doesn't mean you are forgiven
And if you think you're anywhere close
Keep writing because a book is nothing more than a reminder
Of where you failed, and where you need to focus
The life that was versus the life you must lead going forward
Go forward, why don't you
Stop lingering on the past
I dare you to go, and don't tell me you won't look back
Because you will
You always do
Even when there's nothing left

Every Time You're Alone: An Incomplete List

A lane opened, an offering to take a step forward, press down on the gas pedal, up the MPH another fifteen, maybe twenty. But I had been following Red Saturn for the last thirty miles and wasn't yet ready to let go. Red Saturn navigated via the middle lane down the interstate, passing the same exits I passed. I should have pulled over; it was getting dark, yet still early enough to figure out where I'll end up tonight. Red Saturn had its own itinerary. Yes, I knew even then that our camaraderie was silent, entirely imagined. Yet another twenty miles given to our little dance, Red Saturn passing me just as much as I passed it. To the left, and back into the middle; to the right, where we both found that glorious patch of open road, where we could push through those speed traps, passing semi-trucks that made it clear the road was theirs, not ours. Red Saturn pushed south when I went east. I still remember how it felt to finally lose sight of the car.

Between the patch of road shared, we were distantly attuned in the same way you accept the friend request of a stranger, chatting a couple minutes at a time via Facebook chat—you liking my statuses, me doing the same—before disappearing into the newsfeed, the never-ending scroll of this thing we call connection. This feeling, I know, is because of this understanding I recognize that it never gets easier. It never disappears. You could be among friends and family, you could spend a month in the company and drama of others, and still, it waits, a breath caught in your throat, the cough—the rousing and suddenness of remembrance. The feeling, and then the exhale, finally, the recognition that it is temporary but you, you alone, are the sole constant. It was like we never actually met.

5) Outside *Budget Car Rental*, after picking up the Ford Focus, red, go figure, going to stick out, every cop probably noticing the car, fear of being stopped for speeding—never been good at regulating my speed while driving; the moment Jessica, who had graciously driven me from Brooklyn, NY to Trenton, NJ, where the rental awaited, I felt it—the sinking feeling of seeing her drive away, more like her following me as I pulled out of the parking lot, drove back the way we

arrived. Instead of heading south the way I would, she took a different exit, heading back up north, back to the city, back to life itself. I saw her SUV disappear into the traffic. I took one of NJ's famously confusing jughandle exits, vaguely aware I had been too nervous to correctly adjust both rearview and side mirrors, forcing me to drive partially blind, fighting the anxiety of an entire month of this, of driving alone. I should have been familiar with the feeling of being in a car alone, but I wasn't. I can still hear the rapidness of my heartbeat as I merged into the middle lane and accepted that there was no going back.

12) Oh hey, look, just take that rest stop, don't hesitate, Jesus Christ: You can't be sure there'll be another a couple miles down the line. All this coffee, the caffeine low long since become the norm, I parked the car at the other end of the lot, farthest away possible from the building. I was willing to walk the entire length of the lot; I just didn't want to feel smothered by all the other cars parked, side by side, the anxiety of having to eventually pull out of the parking space. It played back in my mind, the situation where I'd mess up, turn too wide, forced to make more than one three-point turn. Or worse, I would collide with a car I didn't see passing by. So I parked the car at the very end, empty spaces on all sides. Leaving the restroom, finally relieved and yet, nothing had changed, I debated getting food. I needed food. But that meant waiting in a longer line than the rest. I opted instead for more coffee. The *Starbucks* line was only three deep. A couple with a young child, couldn't be any older than seven, I eavesdropped the enthusiasm of their trip. They were headed to Florida. Probably the parks, running the usual tourist gauntlet. There was something so calming, so predictable, so... nostalgic about their itinerary. Maybe it was just that they had one, whereas I had no idea where I was going after tomorrow. I thought about just leaving the line and getting back on the road, blast some music, respond to notifications, something, anything, just don't look at me like I'm not supposed to be here.

3) At a bar in Baltimore, before nightfall, first stop on this trip, the trip barely even a thing yet, the messages, the response online minimal, not that I cared if it did—I just needed to see some sort of response, proof that what I was doing was possible. I sipped a whiskey sour, something about the drink tasted odd, or maybe it was just that I was already coming down with the bronchitis didn't know about yet. Michael and Michael chilling, chatting about writing, their works-in-progress, the conversation easy and natural, which is why I stopped in Baltimore: It was safe, familiar, I had lived here for a time, a placed where I had survived a deep depression. And yet, something about it, made itself known when the conversation turned to sports, my attention wavering as their voices rose with excitement and enthusiasm. I couldn't follow—and no harm done, no foul, it was just, oh right, that's it: it was the feeling of being ill-fitting. They might as well have been speaking a different language. But isn't that always the way?

9) Received a text message from someone named Tim, which was encouraging, outright maybe what I needed to hear as I left Baltimore, but I saw it later, much later, long after Tim signed out, maybe unfriended? I'm sorry I didn't reply, and this would be the first of many apologies based around missed connections. I was walking Pittsburgh with friends. Things were starting to look up. I found my second wind. I was not yet suffering from perpetual hangover. I could still taste the food I ate, feel the buzz of a good shot of whiskey. Tim messaged twice, once positive, the other passive aggressive, a simple "well, if you don't feel like it I understand. You're probably too busy to care about my messages." I replied, "Thanks so much! Where do you hail from? I'm headed South, along the east coast. Probably stopping in Atlanta." No reply. When I went back, one late night, in New Orleans, walking back from a bar, I noticed: My message remained unanswered yet had been marked read. Was it something I did, something I said? I don't know you Tim, but maybe my message came off wrong?

22) The walking, always the walking, worse when with the wonderful people that opened their lives to me for the day, day and a half, before I returned to the road, the possibility great this would be all we had, the one time, never again to really communicate, maybe via a comment on Facebook, a DM on Twitter. Maybe they'll post something on Instagram that's funny, a flicker of an interaction, gone before we can even get a sense of where we were coming from; the stroll through a city for the first time, the awe followed by the ache of misunderstanding, the worry that if they weren't there to show me around, I would certainly be that person we passed a few blocks away, lost, asking for directions, with no luck, ignored pleas by the various pedestrians tending to their own lives. On these walks, it starts out the same way: It's fun, engaging, we talk and joke around. I do my best to be present, but soon the pressure to keep in the moment, coupled with the exhaustion and constant glow of my phone, notifications, notifications, more notifications, compromises my attention. I become secondary in the moment, in two places at once. I can tell that my hosts have already pulled back a certain amount of their attention. At its worst, they turn to their own phones. No—even worse than that—they carry conversations where I'm completely excluded from the details. No matter what, it all feels the same.

18) In the waiting room of an urgent care center in Atlanta, GA, perhaps too fixated on the fact the numbing and dull pain in my forehead, I people-watched to prevent from becoming too paranoid from self-diagnosis of my symptoms. Always ends with something far worse than it is—a common cold becomes, I don't know, cancer. Everyone there swimming in the bittersweet delirium of fresh sickness, and the doctors, the entire staff they do their best. How many people pass through those sliding doors daily? How many will recover quickly versus how many will need more help, tests, another doctor, an MRI? The doctor did his best—amicable and almost too kind, but I could tell, I was yet another in the long, never-ending line of patients. How long does it take for a doctor to go numb, grasping finally their job isn't to save but rather silence a patient's suffering, giving them what you can so that maybe it won't be so bad? I walked out into the rain with a prescription and the understanding that I'll be back again, in a different city, a separate time, always, until this body finally gives in, doesn't bounce back, and that's aging, after all, a testament not to "getting old" but rather "getting on" with where we're all going, the one destination we can be sure of.

7) The GPS betrays like anyone and anything else, and when it finally happened, it was appropriately at the worst possible time. Somewhere near Jacksonville, lost along a series of beautiful back roads, I was sure I took the right exit—but maybe not, I don't know, I was following the GPS. The change in scenery delayed the inevitable stress and desperation—the irrational thoughts like "I'm never getting out of this" and "idiot you'll probably end up in Alabama instead of Florida" and then "why Florida—you swore you wouldn't go back"—but soon, the signal nowhere near being re-

covered, the direction nowhere near comprehendible, I pulled the car over. Not a single car in sight, the road merely an echo between grander destinations, I stared off into a field, watching a deer scamper off. I felt so small, the landscape flanking me from all sides. It was good to feel this way; honestly, I was surprised this hadn't dawned on me yet. Odd that I hadn't felt small, like I'm part of a bigger whole—what does this mean about the effects of social media? Pretty sure I already knew before getting into this car. Too busy driving, checking social media, responding to messages and making phone calls. Too busy living in my head. It's a coping mechanism: Living in your head makes it easier to hide from the fact that there is no one in that car with you. There's no one around if you crash. There's no one to really talk to you, even if there is—a phone or text message away—because look, people, like technology, will fail you. The GPS down, Verizon fucking you over, phone signal dead, where is anybody when you need them?

8) Nightfall, more like late night. It was a hotel room, and it was the first in a few times where I broke one of my own rules. In the downpour earlier, there was no choice. I would end up in that cold hotel room, unable to sleep. When I'm unable to sleep, I write. When I can't write, I don't know what I do. I end up downloading Tinder, having downloaded and used it before, but more so in the same way as one does when people-watching, swiping with no intention of ever saying anything. The more you swipe, the more likely you'll find a match; let's say you do. If you don't strike up a conversation, you end up right where you started: a cold hotel room, unable to sleep, staring out the window as another thunderstorm loomed just over the horizon.

39) How often are you able to really enjoy your surroundings—slow down, listen, and take it all in? I had made it to Vegas and spent the night getting lost in the Strip's underground malls with Noah, joking often about the history of Vegas, and more so the simulacrum it had become (maybe always was). Out on the balcony of Noah's apartment, unable to sleep, sitting in a folding chair, I listened not to my thoughts but to all that was around me. In the distance, I heard a police siren, somewhere closer the skittering of a lizard. Despite such disturbances, I was stricken by how quiet it all had become. Someone had turned off the soundtrack to the ever-present anxieties laying any given day. I should have enjoyed this calming moment but instead, the comparisons, the self-judging of the minor inadequacies bubbled back up. This moment should have been mine, a moment of near meditation, instead it slipped through my fingers, ruined.

14) The positive messages and comments work the same as the negative ones: They start out with their intended purposes but soon, almost as soon as the message settles in, it becomes yet another exhale, another feeling lost in translation. Surely it is felt—and appreciated—but so quickly the euphoria that comes from words of encouragement, the sting of a sentence written to explicably hurt you, wears off and you're, once again, looking and responding to others, always others, but maybe not for long. Volume voids out the authenticity of a true connection, and yet, there I was, here I am (there you are?): another notification to replace the one that happened not thirteen seconds ago.

16) Houston, La Quinta, hotel room, punishing sunlight and heat outside, my body either feverish or simply overheated from driving over 40 miles in a car without air conditioning, a car equally on the verge of overheating, and so blink and there was a hotel room.

Blink again and there was a solitary and silent cry. I didn't know how to sit still, to do anything but check my phone, every time I looked at it registered pain, made me nervous, so I reached for the remote, almost forgetting how to watch television. South Park, an episode I had seen before, Stan "growing up"—complete with that overwrought ending scene with Stevie Nicks' voice drowning out any emotion. I remembered this episode, though unsure why it registered such horrible thoughts. I guess it was back when everything around me was ending—friendships, school, hobbies, bands, relationships—and the thought of there being a future was like the open road that still waited for me, another 2000 miles or more to still drive: defined only by all that I had no idea how to define. It wasn't a nervous breakdown because I had lost the nerve of facing the reason why it all became so very much, too much, to handle.

44) New Mexico is gorgeous at sundown. A small little scenic park, vacated at first, until I found a park bench and sat, halving my time between enjoying (or at least trying to enjoy) the sunset and checking notifications/responding to messages. Part of me needed to respond to prevent the information from settling in—the sunset that should be shared is instead my own, and it didn't feel right to think of it as purely for me. Enter someone with their dog, a mix, unsure of which combination of breeds, running up to greet me. It could all be this simple. The owner approached; interacting with other people, I have learned, was never simple. The little chit-chat, mine mostly, spoiled the mood. The sun had set before I could chance a real take, actual enjoyment; petting the dog, I placated the owner, who asked about me, which I gave the minor and maybe fabricated truth. I didn't talk about why I was there, where I was going, or even who I was in favor of chatting about some movie coming out soon, how there'll be another work day tomorrow, and I have always wanted to get another dog, having been without any pets for years, actually since I lived with my ex in Florida. But that's all erased with the depth of a much needed deep sleep, lost to the incoming pressures of yet another long day of driving.

11) Scrolling through social media, seeing the content already posted, recognizing that the trip is almost over, almost done, feeling empty as a result—how is this possible, and for some reason the engagement only makes it feel worse—and yet the taxing of the mind for the next tweet, the next post, further documentation of every possible moment worth the share. I can still see myself in a dozen situations, experiencing it not for the actual experience but for how I would translate it into a post or tweet. Sometimes a person wants nothing else than the safety blanket of their phone; other times, using the phone is a cry for help. Either way, it feels similarly, but the same could be said for being in the throes of a conversation where you cannot keep up, cannot fully connect, swimming upstream, the current too incompatible and imbalanced to fall in line.

25) Waiting for a podcast to start, watching Matt scroll through his purchased movies on Apple TV, which I should have enjoyed, but the fact that this had to become a podcast, how I would have to be a version of myself less than authentic, for virtue of the podcast's theme and purpose, the end result I still haven't listened to. You might never be alone in enjoying success, people appearing from all corners to congratulate, but when you bomb, when you fail, when you visibly missed the mark, you truly feel the distance between you and someone else. Would-be heightened senses, you refuse to acknowledge how vulnerable it feels. Even if you could hide, you still need to do all the hiding, and in those shadows, the only person you can trust to be there is yourself. How brutal is that?

15) Still sitting in the driver's seat, same posture and same relative stress as before but now in a different time zone, the opposite coast, the same company, but instead of picking up, I was now dropping off. The car. A quick check of the condition of the vehicle, followed by my own documenting of the mileage, the way the car looked as I removed all of my belongings—tossing out a month's worth of beef jerky and empty energy drinks, finding it all so convenient that in seeing again that one granola bar wrapper in the back seat, it reminded me of that one gas station in West Virginia where I was passed over in line by two separate customers, the cashier ignoring me for reasons I can assume but will never fully know. The flashes of each occurrence are quick to leave, just as I am quick to walk away from the car, calling an Uber that will send me into the depths of downtown Portland, and yet I don't look back at the car. I don't look back because I was unable to process my feelings. So strange to develop a connection to an object, to apply meaning and memory to things, especially when you know they are not long for your life, not yours to have and take with you. But then why does it feel like by leaving it behind, I was leaving behind part of myself?

20) Beware Twitter DMs, your Facebook Messenger—not necessarily for its contents, but sure, why not? More so, the warning is saved for all that you might never see, all the ones I'll never open, left unread, the notice that the interactions have slowed down, naturally because it's almost over, understanding that when they speed back up, I'll push away, always pushing away, and why is that? Why can't I grasp the idea that these are people going out of their way to chat, they could easily not. And in some remote corner of the mind is a worry that one day that'll happen. It's so sad to place so much value on that validation.

57) Portland, morning, the last morning, day 30 of 30, Uber driver alarmingly friendly. We get to talking about social media—he had helped his brother launch his own clothing brand, and it was growing in popularity. The driver discussed how grassroots promotions really helped and how his brother had capitalized on Instagram. I reciprocated, discussing this trip, much to his curiosity and constant inquiries. At first I enjoyed our discussion, but soon, I felt sorry for him, aware that at two separate junctures, he turned away from the turn the app had suggested, causing us to travel through a much more circuitous route. No big deal, he meant well, yet how dare I feel sorry for him? It was not my right, nor my business to assume, much less apply such a dreaded feeling as pity to someone I didn't know. I probably needed this drive more than he did. I needed to unload my excitement and frustration about the technology. Maybe he simply didn't know the city well, bad with directions; maybe his own GPS was malfunctioning, *as they often do*. When he dropped me off, he repeated his name twice, shook my hand, and wished me well. I did the same, well, the last part. I wished him well.

29) Writing while on the road, be it the dispatches for Fanzine, lengthy email responses to those supporting the trip, or taking copious amounts of notes for the book to come later: I was forced to take a step back and reflect, see the demons defined even before I can make sense of what and where (and why) they might have risen, chosen to exist. When it's a constant drive to move forward, the fixation on meeting those goals, the inert moments spent staring at a screen remind of all the hours, all the days, the months in figurative seclusion, all the sentences written that'll never be read, and all the books published that'll never reach any more than a handful. And yet it's still in the act of solitude that I look to make a connection, to be something other than alone. There's something so broken about it, but look, I'm still here. I'm writing in the darkness of a room, shortly after dusk.

19) Not the redeye or the airport itself, but really the drive to the airport. Kevin in the driver seat, Katie and I to be both dropped off—her headed to Sewanee, me headed back to NYC—we chatted like it wouldn't be long, both of us back in Portland tomorrow, if not then maybe the day after. Yet none of us knew when we'd all be back in the same city again. I say this more for myself, being driven to PDX as the day ended, the long night ahead, I would arrive on the east coast just as another began, with the same worries I carried with me all month. In equal doses, so much had changed and yet maybe not much at all. I still had another essay to write, another dozen deadlines, a job search, a life to once again rebuild after having seen it fall apart in the month(s) leading up to the trip. I returned to New York City in pieces, no different than when I had moved there, a little over a year ago.

1) I can't go on, and like the famous Beckett quote, I will go on. I mean, I already have. More a beginning than an ending, I could add in the writing of this essay another notch, another number to the counting. But instead I'll crawl out of this quiet moment, and let it settle. If you don't look out the window, you forget what is worth seeing. A person could get used to anything. I find it so ironic that the only way I can write about loneliness is when I'm right in the middle of it.

This essay was originally published by Berfrois

Michael J Seidlinger is an Asian American author of a number of novels including *My Pet Serial Killer*, *The Fun We've Had* and *The Strangest*. He serves as the social media editor at Electric Literature, a producer for Publishers Weekly, and co-publisher of Civil Coping Mechanisms. You can find him online on Facebook, Twitter (@mjseidlinger), and Instagram (@michaelseidlinger). He lives in Brooklyn, New York, where he never sleeps and is forever searching for the next best cup of coffee.

Other titles from Broken River Books:

Zero Saints by Gabino Iglesias

Black Gum by J David Osborne

Graveyard Love by Scott Adlerberg

The Heartbeat Harvest by Mark Jaskowski

Chupacabra Vengeance by David Bowles

Heathenish by Kelby Losack

Gravity by Michael Kazepis

Hard Sentences: Crime Fiction Inspired by Alcatraz
edited by
David James Keaton & Joe Clifford

The Snake Handler by Cody Goodfellow
& J David Osborne

Human Trees by Matthew Revert

Itzá by Rios de la Luz

Jack Waters by Scott Adlerberg

For more information on Broken River Books,
please visit:
www.brokenriverbooks.com

Follow us on Twitter: @brbjdo
Follow us on Instagram: @brbjdo

Made in United States
Orlando, FL
01 July 2025

62557181R00080